Published by
Winston Press,
430 Oak Grove, Minneapolis, MN 55403

Original edition published in English
under the title More Precious Than Gold
by Lion Publishing, England.
Copyright © 1985. All rights reserved.

ISBN 0-86683-845-7 (previously ISBN: 0-85648-568-3)

Compiled by Ruth Connell

Printed in Great Britain

MORE PRECIOUS THAN GOLD

Psalm 19

Winston Press

*T*he heavens declare the glory of God;
the skies proclaim the work of his hands.
Day after day they pour forth speech;
night after night they display knowledge.
There is no speech or language where their voice
is not heard.
Their voice goes out into all the earth,
their words to the ends of the world.
In the heavens he has pitched a tent for the sun,
which is like a bridegroom coming forth
from his pavilion,
like a champion rejoicing to run his course.
It rises at one end of the heavens
and makes its circuit to the other;
nothing is hidden from its heat.
The law of the Lord is perfect, reviving the soul.
The statutes of the Lord are trustworthy,
making wise the simple.
The precepts of the Lord are right,
giving joy to the heart.
The commands of the Lord are radiant,
giving light to the eyes.

The fear of the Lord is pure, enduring for ever.
The ordinances of the Lord are sure
and altogether righteous.
They are more precious than gold,
than much pure gold;
they are sweeter than honey,
than honey from the comb.
By them is your servant warned;
in keeping them there is great reward.
Who can discern his errors?
Forgive my hidden faults.
Keep your servant also from wilful sins;
may they not rule over me.
Then will I be blameless,
innocent of great transgression.
May the words of my mouth and the meditation
of my heart
be pleasing in your sight,
O Lord, my Rock and my Redeemer.

Psalm 19

*T*he heavens declare the glory of God

In the beginning God created the heavens and the earth . . . And God said, 'Let there be lights in the firmament of the heavens to separate the day from the night; and let them be for signs and for seasons and for days and years, and let them be lights in the firmament of the heavens to give light upon the earth.' And it was so. And God made the two great lights, the greater light to rule the day, and the lesser light to rule the night; he made the stars also. And God set them in the firmament of the heavens to give light upon the earth, to rule over the day and over the night, and to separate the light from the darkness. And God saw that it was good.

Genesis 1:1,14–18

When we behold the heavens, when we contemplate the celestial bodies, can we fail of conviction? Must we not acknowledge that there is a divinity, a perfect being, a ruling intelligence, which governs; a God who is everywhere and directs all by his power? Anybody who doubts this may as well deny there is a sun that lights us.

Cicero

When I look at thy heavens, the work of thy fingers, the moon and the stars which thou hast established; what is man that thou art mindful of him, and the son of man that thou dost care for him?

Psalm 8:3–4

*T*he skies proclaim the work of his hands

All the creatures of your universe join in an unending chorus of praise . . . When our souls become depressed, they find sympathetic support in the things you have created, and so are lifted up to you, the marvellous Creator of everything.

Augustine

The more I study nature, the more I am amazed at the Creator.

Louis Pasteur

Though we speak much we cannot reach the end,
and the sum of our words is:
'He is the all.'
Where shall we find strength to praise him?
For he is greater than all his works.

Ecclesiasticus 43:27–28

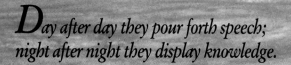

Day after day they pour forth speech;
night after night they display knowledge.

The more we learn about the wonders of the universe, the more
clearly we are going to perceive the hand of God.
Frank Borman

The whole world is nothing else but God expressed.
John Boys

God, who created the universe, sustains it by his power, and governs
every part of it by his providence . . . No man seriously believes that
God created all things, unless he believes that God cares continually
for all things that he has created.
John Calvin

In these last days God has spoken to us by a Son, whom he appointed the heir of all things, through whom also he created the world. He reflects the glory of God and bears the very stamp of his nature, upholding the universe by his word of power.

Hebrews 1:2–3

*T*here is no speech or language where their voice is not heard. Their voice goes out into all the earth, their words to the ends of the world.

Sun, moon and stars are God's travelling preachers.

Charles Haddon Spurgeon

Since the creation of the world God's invisible qualities – his eternal power and divine nature – have been clearly seen, being understood from what has been made, so that men are without any excuse.

Romans 1:20

Always, everywhere God is present, and always he seeks to discover himself. To each one he would reveal not only that he is, but what he is as well.

A. W. Tozer

As there is but one God and Father of us all, whose glory gives light and life to everything that lives, whose presence fills all places, whose power supports all beings, whose providence ruleth all events; so everything that lives, whether in heaven or earth . . . must all, with one spirit, live wholly to the praise and glory of this one God and Father of them all.

William Law

You are worthy, our Lord and God,
to receive glory and honour and power,
for you created all things,
and by your will they were created and have their being.

Revelation 4:11

In the heavens he has pitched a tent for the sun, which is like a bridegroom coming forth from his pavilion, like a champion rejoicing to run his course.

Praised be my Lord God for all his creatures, especially for our brother the sun, who brings us the day and who brings us the light; fair is he and shines with a very great splendour; O Lord, he signifies you to us!

Francis of Assisi

No other creature yields such joy to the earth as her bridegroom the sun; and none, whether they be horse or eagle, can for an instant compare in swiftness with that heavenly champion.

Charles Haddon Spurgeon

The sun, which is the light and strength and joy of natural existence, shines for the believer with a splendour not its own. For by faith he understands creation.

Arthur Pridham

It rises at one end of the heavens and makes its circuit to the other; nothing is hidden from its heat.

Pride of the heights, shining vault,
so, in a glorious spectacle, the sky appears.
The sun, as he emerges, proclaims at his rising,
'A thing of wonder is the work of the Most High!'
At his zenith he parches the land,
who can withstand his blaze?
A man must blow a furnace to produce any heat,
the sun burns the mountains three times as much;
breathing out blasts of fire,
flashing his rays he dazzles the eyes.
Great is the Lord who made him,
and whose word speeds him on his course.

Ecclesiasticus 43:1–5

I am the Lord, and there is no other;
apart from me there is no God.
I will strengthen you,
though you have not acknowledged me,
so that from the rising of the sun
to the place of its setting
men may know there is none besides me.
I am the Lord, and there is no other.

Isaiah 45:5–6

Who is God, but the Lord? . . . You are unchanging yet you change everything. You are never new, never old; yet you make all things new.

Augustine

The law of the Lord is perfect, reviving the soul.

The order of the divine mind, embodied in the divine law, is beautiful. What should a man do but try to reproduce it, so far as possible, in his daily life?

C. S. Lewis

God's glory, that is, his goodness, appears much in the works of creation, but much more in and by divine revelation.

Matthew Henry

The moral law . . . is the heart of God disclosed to man.

John Wesley

To keep God's testimonies is at once the consequence and the proof of seeking him with whole-hearted devotion and determination. To walk in his ways is the preservative from evil-doing.

Alexander MacLaren

God, by your law we are called back to you, through a mixture of the wholesome, the bitter, from the destructive delights that once pulled us away from you.

Augustine

*T*he statutes of the Lord are trustworthy, making wise the simple.

God's laws have 'truth', intrinsic validity, rock-bottom reality, being rooted in his own nature, and are therefore as solid as that nature which he has created.

C. S. Lewis

Those that are humbly simple, this is, sensible of their own folly, and willing to be taught, those shall be made wise by the Word of God.

Matthew Henry

Good and upright is the Lord;
therefore he instructs sinners in the way.
He leads the humble in what is right,
and teaches the humble his way.

Psalm 25:8–9

The law was our school-master to bring us unto Christ, that we might be justified by faith.

Galatians 3:24

---

*T*he precepts of the Lord are right,
giving joy to the heart.

The law itself is righteousness, filling the soul with a peace which passeth all understanding, and causing us to rejoice evermore, in the testimony of a good conscience toward God.

John Wesley

If a man loves you he should find joy above all else in the fulfilment in his own life of your will and everlasting decree.

Thomas à Kempis

There is no gladness equal to that of knowing and doing the will of God.

Alexander MacLaren

Blessed is the man whom thou shalt instruct, Lord; and shalt teach him out of thy law. This is not a schooling which enlightens the mind only; it also warms the heart.

Thomas Aquinas

---

*You are good, and what you do is good;
teach me your decrees.*

Psalm 119:68

*T*he commands of the Lord are radiant,
giving light to the eyes.

Thy word is a lamp to my feet
and a light to my path.

Psalm 119:105

It is the ordinary means which the Spirit useth in 'enlightening the
eyes'; it brings us a sight and sense of our sin and misery and directs
us in the way of duty.

Matthew Henry

I would not have known what sin was except through the law. For I
would not have known what it was to covet if the law had not said,
'Do not covet.'

Paul, in Romans 7:7

The law moves those that are subject to it to act aright.

Thomas Aquinas

---

*T*he fear of the Lord is pure, enduring for ever.

Where there is the fear of the Lord to guard the house the enemy cannot find a way to enter.

Francis of Assisi

Right fear . . . begetteth and continueth in the soul a great reverence of God, his word and his ways; keeping it tender, and making it afraid to turn from them, to the right hand or to the left, to anything that may dishonour God, break its peace, grieve the Spirit, or cause the enemy to speak reproachfully.

John Bunyan, from 'The Pilgrim's Progress'

Fear God, and keep his commandments;
for this is the whole duty of man.

Ecclesiastes 12:13

Jesus said: 'You shall love the Lord your God with all your heart, and with all your soul, and with all your mind. This is the great and first commandment. And a second is like it, You shall love your neighbour as yourself. On these two commandments depend all the law and the prophets.'

Matthew 22:37–40

The fear of the Lord is the beginning of knowledge.

Proverbs 1:7

The ordinances of the Lord are sure and altogether righteous.

The law is in the highest degree pure, chaste, clean and holy. Otherwise it could not be the immediate offspring, and much less the express resemblance, of God, who is essential holiness.

John Wesley

The law is holy, and the commandment is holy and just and good.

Romans 7:12

The only way a man can lose you is to leave you; and if he leaves you, where does he go? He can run only from your pleasure to your wrath. Where does he end up without finding your law fulfilled in his punishment? Your law is the truth and you are the truth.

Augustine

Jesus said to his disciples, 'Think not that I have come to abolish the law and the prophets; I have come not to abolish them but to fulfil them. For truly, I say to you, till heaven and earth pass away, not an iota, not a dot, will pass from the law until all is accomplished. Whoever then relaxes one of the least of these commandments and teaches men so, shall be called least in the kingdom of heaven; but he who does them and teaches them shall be called great in the kingdom of heaven.

Matthew 5:17–19

The law by which God rules us, is as dear to him as the gospel by which he saves us.

William Secker

They are more precious than gold, than much pure gold;
they are sweeter than honey, than honey from the comb.

To him who tastes God, all the sweetness of the world will be but bitterness.
Francis of Assisi

The psalmist had often brooded on the thought of what the law was, because, loving its giver, he must needs love the gift.

The law . . . is not harsh, but glowing with love, God's best gift.
Alexander MacLaren

*B*y them is your servant warned

Every law that God has given has been for man's benefit. If man breaks it, he is not only rebelling against God, he is hurting himself.
Billy Graham

The law shows us our sinfulness and misery of our departures from God, and the indispensable necessity of our return to him.
Matthew Henry

All Scripture is inspired by God and profitable for teaching, for reproof, for correction, and for training in righteousness, that the man of God may be equipped for every good work.
2 Timothy 3:16–17

In keeping them there is great reward

In the perfect and eternal world the law will vanish, but the results of having lived faithfully under it will not.
C. S. Lewis

The rich reward consists in no outward advantage but in the simple observance of God's law; rich it is, because its very exercise is joy.
Augustine

Jesus said: 'If you keep my commandments, you will abide in my love, just as I have kept my Father's commandments and abide in his love.'
John 15:10

He who walks in God's law walks in God's company, and he must be blessed.

Charles Haddon Spurgeon

Behold, I am coming soon! My reward is with me, and I will give to everyone according to what he has done. I am the Alpha and the Omega, the First and the Last, the Beginning and the End.

Revelation 22:12–13

Who can discern his errors?
Forgive my hidden faults.

As he (the psalmist) has felt the sun, perhaps in the desert, searching him out in every nook of shade where he attempted to hide from it, so he feels the law searching out all the hiding-places of his soul.

C. S. Lewis

God knows a great deal more evil by us than we do ourselves. In many things we all offend, and who can tell how often he offends?

Matthew Henry

Whether I am alone, or seen of men, I do all my actions in the sight of God, who must judge them.

Blaise Pascal

Hear me, O God. Alas for man's sin! When a man speaks in that way you have mercy on him, Lord, because you made man and not the sin in him.

Augustine

If we confess our sins, he is faithful and just, and will forgive our sins and cleanse us from all unrighteousness.

1 John 1:9

---

*If you, O Lord, kept a record of sins,
O Lord, who could stand?
But with you there is forgiveness;
therefore you are feared.*

Psalm 130:3

---

*K*eep your servant also from wilful sins; may they
not rule over me.
Then will I be blameless, innocent of great
transgression.

I find it to be a law that when I want to do right, evil lies close at
hand. For I delight in the law of God, in my inmost self, but I see in
my members another law at war with the law of my mind and
making me captive to the law of sin which dwells in my members.
Wretched man that I am! Who will deliver me from this body of
death? Thanks be to God through Jesus Christ our Lord!

Romans 7:21–25

When unrighteousness had come to its full term, and it had become
perfectly plain that its recompense of punishment and death had to be
expected, then the season arrived in which God had determined to
show henceforth his goodness and power. O the overflowing
kindness and love of God toward man! God did not hate us, or drive
us away, or bear us ill will. Rather, he was long-suffering and
forbearing. In his mercy, he took up the burden of our sins. He
himself gave up his own Son as a ransom for us – the holy one for the
unjust, the innocent for the guilty, the righteous one for the
unrighteous, the incorruptible for the corruptible, the immortal for
the mortal. For what else could cover our sins except his
righteousness? In whom could we, lawless and impious as we were,
be made righteous except in the Son of God alone?

Letter to Diognetus

When the time had fully come, God sent forth his Son, born of woman, born under the law, to redeem those who were under the law, so that we might receive adoption as sons. And because you are sons, God has sent the Spirit of his Son into our hearts, crying, 'Abba! Father!' So through God you are no longer a slave but a son, and if a son then an heir.

Galatians 4:4–7

May the words of my mouth and the meditation of my heart be pleasing in your sight, O Lord, my Rock and my Redeemer.

Make time to attend to your inner life, and frequently think over the benefits God has given you.

Thomas à Kempis

There is not in the world a way of life more sweet, nor more delightful than continued converse with God. Those only who practise it, and savour it, can understand it.

Brother Lawrence

We have reason for believing that our prayers will be heard when the words of the mouth truly express the meditation of the heart. Too often the words are right, and the meditation wrong.

Graham Scroggie

Prayer is the act by which we divest ourselves of all false belongings and become free to belong to God and God alone.

Henri Nouwen

What is the chief end of man?
Man's chief end is to glorify God,
and to enjoy him for ever.

Shorter Westminster Catechism

Prayer

O God, who art nigh to all them
that call upon thee in truth;
who art thyself the Truth,
whom to know is perfect knowledge:
Instruct us with thy divine wisdom,
and teach us thy law;
that we may know the truth and walk in it;
through him in whom the truth was made manifest,
even Jesus Christ, thy Son, our Lord.

Based on a prayer by Augustine

---

*Quotations from copyright material are as
follows:*
Augustine, The Confessions of Augustine in
Modern English, *translated by Sherwood E.
Wirt, Zondervan Publishers 1971, Lion
Publishing 1978; C. E. B. Cranfield,* The First
Epistle of Peter, *SCM Press 1950; Thomas à
Kempis,* The Imitation of Christ, *translated by
Betty I. Knott, Collins Fontana 1963; Brother
Lawrence,* The Practice of the Presence of
God, *translated by E. M. Blaiklock, Hodder
and Stoughton 1981; C. S. Lewis,* Reflections
on the Psalms, *Geoffrey Bles 1958; Henri
Nouwen, quoted in* Waging Peace, *Harper and
Row 1983; Graham Scroggie,* Know Your
Bible: Psalms, *Pickering and Inglis 1948; A. W.
Tozer,* The Pursuit of God, *Christian
Publications 1948, Marshall, Morgan and Scott
1961*

—Picture Acknowledgements—
*—Famous Passages: More Precious Than
Gold—*

*Photographs by Sonia Halliday Photographs:
Sister Daniel, page 33, Sonia Halliday, pages
36–37, Martine Klotz, page 10; Lion
Publishing: David Alexander, page 38, Jon
Willcocks, pages 16, 19, 20, 22, 41; Jean-Luc
Ray, pages 15, 34; ZEFA, pages 5, 9, 12–13, 25,
26, 29, 30, 42–43 and cover*